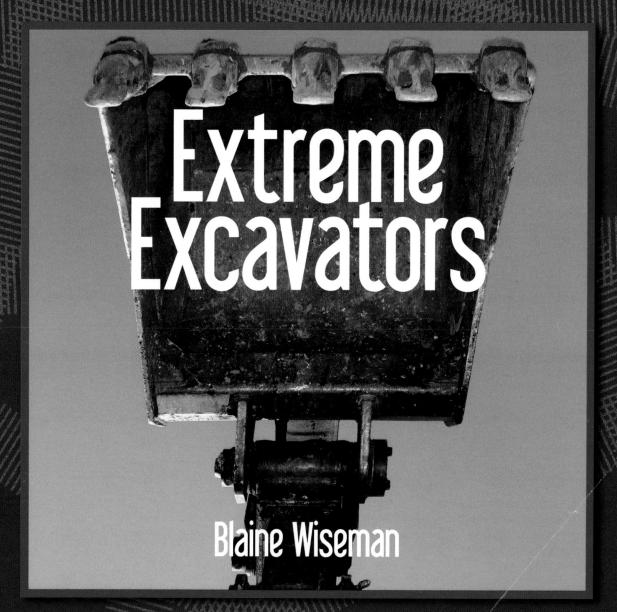

Extreme Excavators

Blaine Wiseman

WEIGL PUBLISHERS INC.
"Creating Inspired Learning"
www.weigl.com

Published by Weigl Publishers Inc.
350 5th Avenue, 59th Floor
New York, NY 10118
Website: www.weigl.com

Library of Congress Cataloging-in-Publication Data

Wiseman, Blaine.
 Excavators : WOW big machines / Blaine Wiseman.
     p. cm.
 Includes index.
 ISBN 978-1-61690-133-2 (hardcover : alk. paper) -- ISBN 978-1-61690-134-9 (softcover : alk. paper) -- ISBN 978-1-61690-135-6 (e-book)
 1. Earthmoving machinery--Juvenile literature. I. Title.
 TA725.W55 2011
 624.1'52--dc22
                                        2010013935

Printed in the United States of America in North Mankato, Minnesota
2 3 4 5 6 7 8 9 0 15 14 13 12 11

022011
WEP040211

Editor: Heather C. Hudak
Design: Terry Paulhus

All of the Internet URLs given in the book were valid at the time of publication. However, due to the dynamic nature of the Internet, some addresses may have changed, or sites may have ceased to exist since publication. While the author and publisher regret any inconvenience this may cause readers, no responsibility for any such changes can be accepted by either the author or the publisher.

Every reasonable effort has been made to trace ownership and to obtain permission to reprint copyright material. The publishers would be pleased to have any errors or omissions brought to their attention so that they may be corrected in subsequent printings.

Weigl acknowledges Getty Images as its primary image supplier for this title.

CONTENTS

What are Excavators?

Have you ever wondered how basements are made? Excavators can be used to dig holes for basements. An excavator is a big machine that has a large bucket at the end of a long arm. The arm is attached to a **cab** that can spin around. The cab is called the house, and it sits on top of wheels or tracks.

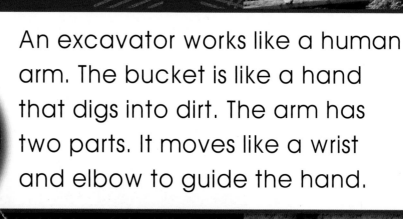

An excavator works like a human arm. The bucket is like a hand that digs into dirt. The arm has two parts. It moves like a wrist and elbow to guide the hand.

5

Dig a Hole

What is an excavator's job? Excavators dig huge holes. They take material out of the ground. Some excavators dig holes that are thousands of feet (meters) deep.

Excavators use their bucket to dig holes. Metal teeth at the end of the bucket scrape and dig at the ground. The bucket fills with dirt, rocks, and other objects. When it is full, the driver in the cab swings the arm and dumps the objects.

Tracks or Wheels

What do excavators have in common with tanks? They both move on **tracks**. Excavators that have tracks are sometimes called crawlers. Crawlers are more common than excavators with wheels.

Tracks are better than wheels for moving on rocky dirt roads. However, wheel excavators can move faster than crawlers.

About the Arm

How does an excavator's arm work? There are two main parts that make up the arm. The part closest to the house is called the boom. Mono booms are only able to move up and down. Knuckle booms can move up and down, as well as left to right.

The stick is the part of the arm that is attached to the boom. It has a joint like a person's elbow. The stick gives the excavator the power to pull the bucket through the dirt.

Where Does It Go?

What makes excavator arms move? Excavators get their power from hydraulics. This is a system that pushes oil from one tube to another. This action creates power in another part of the machine. Hydraulics turn a small amount of energy into a large amount of power.

New, environmentally friendly systems use less fuel to power machines. Saving fuel helps the environment. It also means less pollution is sent into the air in the form of **exhaust**.

Dig, Push, and Break

Did you know that the bucket of an excavator can be removed? The bucket can be replaced with an auger or a breaker. An auger is a spiral-shaped blade that spins. It digs narrow holes for planting trees and posts in the ground. A breaker works like a **jackhammer**. It breaks apart hard objects, such as concrete or rocks.

Many excavators have a blade. This large, metal blade attaches to the front of the excavator below the house. It is used to push objects around. It can be used to make the ground smooth.

15

Sticks and Sensors

Did you know that **joysticks** are used to move the parts of an excavator? Drivers use many joysticks and sensors to move the bucket, stick, boom, house, and tracks or wheels. Each movement of the joystick causes a part of the excavator to move in a different direction.

Excavators are used to **level** land. When the bucket reaches a certain height, a system of sensors tells the driver to stop digging. These sensors use lasers and **GPS**.

Big Buckets

What are the world's biggest machines? Bucket-wheel excavators are the biggest land-based vehicles. They have several buckets on a spinning wheel at the end of the arm. These buckets can remove large amounts of material at once.

The biggest bucket-wheel excavator stands 312 feet (95 meters) tall. This big machine has 20 buckets.

Land Use

Did you know that excavators can help the environment? Excavators are used at **landfills** to dig large holes in the ground. Garbage and waste are then pushed into the holes and covered with dirt.

Over time, the land that has been covered over can be reused. This land is clean and free from waste. Many communities, golf courses, and parks have been built on top of old landfills.

Handheld Hydraulics

Two small pumps with a plunger

Water

Plastic tube

1. With an adult's help, push in the plungers of both pumps as far as they can go.

2. Fill one pump with water. To do this, place the tip of the pump in the water. Then, pull up slowly on the plunger.

3. Fit the nozzle of each pump into either side of the plastic tube. Make sure both ends are airtight.

4. Push the water out of the full pump. What happens to the other pump?

5. Now, push the other pump's plunger. This is how hydraulics work.

Find Out More

To learn more about excavators, visit these websites.

How Stuff Works
www.howstuffworks.com/hydraulic.htm

Discovery Channel
www.yourdiscovery.
com/greatest_ever/
construction_machines

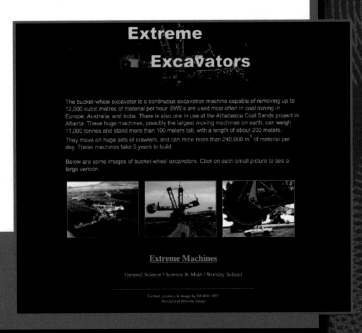

Extreme Excavators
www.worsleyschool.net/science/
files/extreme/excavators.html

Glossary

cab: the place on a vehicle where the driver sits

exhaust: the waste from burning fuel

GPS: Global Positioning System; a system that uses satellites and a receiver to identify an exact location

jackhammer: a tool that moves up and down very fast to break apart hard objects

joysticks: rod-shaped control sticks used to move machines

landfills: places where people in a city or town take their trash

level: to make the ground even

tracks: endless belts that move over rough ground

Index